© TONY CAMPBELL - FOTOLIA

© JOËL BEHR - FOTOLIA

© ELENATHEWISE - FOTOLIA

© ANDY - FOTOLIA

© KUSHNIROV AVRAHAM - FOTOLIA

© ZIGGY - FOTOLIA

© PETER WEY - FOTOLIA

© WIREPEC - FOTOLIA

© DENNIS BURNS - ISTOCKPHOTO

GENERAL DIRECTOR: GAUTHIER AUZOU
SENIOR EDITOR: GWENAËLLE HAMON
JUNIOR EDITOR: LESLY CARRER
ILLUSTRATIONS: OLIVIER VERBRUGGHE, CLAIRE VOGEL AND MARCO FERRARIS
PHOTOGRAPHS: FRONT ENDS © MARTIN M303 - FOTOLIA, BACK ENDS © DENNIS BURNS - ISTOCKPHOTO

LAYOUT: ANNAÏS TASSONE
ENGLISH VERSION EDITOR: CHRISTOPHER MURRAY
TRANSLATION FROM FRENCH: SUSAN ALLEN MAURIN
CONSULTANT: PATRICK DAVID (NATURALIST)
PRODUCTION: AMANDINE DUREL

© AUZOU PUBLISHING, PARIS (FRANCE), 2013 (ENGLISH VERSION)
ISBN: 978-2-7338-2315-6

PRINTED AND BOUND IN CHINA, SEPTEMBER 2013

MY BOOK OF ANIMALS

A WALK THROUGH THE NATIONAL PARKS

CONTENTS

DESERT ANIMALS

THE COYOTE

Identity Card

32 – 37 in.
(81 – 94 cm)

20 – 50 lbs.
(9 – 23 kg)

● Yellowstone National Park, Wyoming, Montana and Idaho
■ Zone range

WHAT IS IT?

The COYOTE is a cousin of the wolf and is extremely fast. It is a slender animal with a pointed nose, long, thin legs, and a gray or tawny-colored coat.

WHERE DOES IT LIVE AND WHAT DOES IT EAT?

The COYOTE can be found in deserts and steppes as well as in chaparrals, prairies, swamps, and forests. It lives in packs like the wolf but it hunts alone. It is a formidable predator that feeds on a variety of small animals.

WHAT IS THE ORIGIN OF ITS NAME?

The name COYOTE comes from a Native American word that means "the one that howls." It is true that at night, the howls of this animal are both eerie and loud.

USEFUL TO KNOW...

The COYOTE is still very common. It will approach houses, even in big cities, in search of food. If it feels threatened, it can attack.

PLAY AND LEARN!

The COYOTE lives in the desert.

- True

- False

It is a cousin of the cat.

- True

- False

It howls loudly at night.

- True

- False

It lives alone.

- True

- False

Identity Card

 9 – 15 in. (shell length)
(23 – 38 cm)

8 – 15 lbs.
(3.5 – 7 kg)

● Joshua Tree National Park, California
▪ Zone range

WHAT IS IT?

It has a high-domed shell, or carapace, that is greenish to dark brown in color. With heavy, claw-like scales, its front limbs are well designed for digging.

WHERE DOES IT LIVE?

It lives in a variety of habitats from sandy flats to rocky foothills and canyons. Its diet includes herbs, grasses, some shrubs, and the new growth of cacti.

DID YOU KNOW...

Adult DESERT TORTOISES do not need to drink much because they can survive a year or more without access to water! They just find the necessary water in their food.

CAN YOU EASILY FIND A DESERT TORTOISE?

It is one of the most elusive inhabitants of the desert, spending up to 95% of its time underground to escape the heat of summer and the cold of winter. They live deep in burrows and will spend the winter months in a torpid or dormant state.

PLAY AND LEARN!

How is the **DESERT TORTOISE's shell?**

• In the form of a dome

• With two humps

• With several humps

It eats mainly...

• Little insects

• Grass and herbs

• Mice

What color can be its shell?

• Bright yellow

• Brown

• Red

THE KANGAROO RAT

Identity Card

3.5 – 5.5 in.
(9 cm – 14 cm)

up to 4.5 oz.
(130 grams)

● Great Sand Dunes National Park, Colorado
■ Zone range

■ WHAT IS IT?

The KANGAROO RAT is a small rodent that has a long tail (5.5 to 6 inches long – 14 cm-15.5 cm) and big hind feet with four toes. They have large heads with big eyes and small ears. They like to eat seeds.

■ WHERE DOES IT LIVE?

KANGAROO RATS generally live in underground burrows they excavated themselves. They spend the day in their burrow and go out at night — when the temperature is cooler — to eat.

■ DID YOU KNOW...

The life span of KANGAROO RATS is very short, from two to five years.

■ WHAT IS THE ORIGIN OF THEIR NAMES?

Just like the kangaroos in Australia, most KANGAROO RATS hop on their hind feet, using their tails for balance, and have pouches to carry food back to their burrows.

PLAY AND LEARN!

KANGAROO RATS carry their babies in their pouches.

- True
- False

They have only four toes on each foot.

- True
- False

They like to eat seeds.

- True
- False

They have a short tail.

- True
- False

Identity Card

Up to 1 ft. 8 in. in length
(55 cm)

Up to 5.5 lbs.
(2.5 kg)

• Joshua Tree National Park, California
■ Zone range

WHAT IS IT?

The JACKRABBIT is not a wild rabbit; its hind feet are longer. It has a brown coat in the summer but in the winter, its fur turns white.

HOW DOES IT LIVE?

The JACKRABBIT lives alone on its territory. It feeds on grass and plants. The female hare, the doe, gives birth to about 20 leverets a year.

WHERE DOES IT LIVE?

It lives in big forests, thickets and understories — which are the parts of the forest that are under the leaves but above the ground. It does not dig a den but shelters itself under the vegetation in a hideout called a "form."

IS IT FAST?

Thanks to its muscular hind feet, it can reach 28 mph (45 km/h) and jump to a height of 9 ft. 10 in. (3 meters)!

PLAY AND LEARN!

The JACKRABBIT digs deep dens.

• True

• False

It lives mostly in forests.

• True

• False

It jumps high thanks to its long tail.

• True

• False

It turns white in winter.

• True

• False

THE RAVEN

Identity Card

24 – 26 in.
(60 – 66 cm)

2.3 lbs
(1 kg)

● Bryce Canyon National Park, Utah
■ Zone range

WHAT IS IT?

The RAVEN is a bird that has long and black feathers. They are excellent and acrobatic fliers on a par with falcons and hawks.

HOW DO RAVENS LIVE?

The RAVEN eats everything it can find. Therefore, its food will change from season to season, and include insects, cereals, fruits, little reptiles, etc.

DID YOU KNOW...

RAVENS are effective hunters. Sometimes they use cooperative techniques. That is to say RAVENS team up to hunt down game too large for a single bird.

DO THEY LIVE IN A LARGE GROUP?

In winter, RAVENS may gather in flocks to forage during the day and to roost at night. During the rest of the year, they are often coupled, or in small groups. They build large, stick nests in which females lay three to seven eggs each spring.

PLAY AND LEARN!

RAVENS have...

- white feathers

- red feathers

- black feathers

What do they eat?

- only insects

- everything they can find

- fish

How many eggs can they have?

- only one

- three

- fifteen

Identity Card

20 – 24 in.
(50 – 61 cm)

17 – 24 lbs
(7.5 – 11 kg)

• Death Valley National Park, California and Nevada
▪ Zone range

WHAT IS IT?

The ROADRUNNER is a long-legged bird with a distinctive head crest.

WHAT DOES IT EAT?

The ROADRUNNER feeds on insects, fruit, and seeds, small reptiles (including snakes), small mammals, spiders, scorpions, centipedes, small birds and bird eggs, and even dead animals.

WHERE DOES ITS NAME COME FROM?

Its name comes from the bird's habit of racing down roads in front of moving vehicles and then darting to safety in the bush.

WHAT DOES IT DO WHEN IT FEELS DANGER?

When the ROADRUNNER senses danger or is traveling downhill, it flies, revealing short, rounded wings. But it cannot keep its large body airborne for more than a few seconds, and so prefers walking or running.

PLAY AND LEARN!

ROADRUNNERS fly very well.

• True

• False

Its name comes from the fact that it can run as fast as a car.

• True

• False

It has long legs.

• True

• False

It has a crest on its head.

• True

• False

THE SIDEWINDER

Identity Card

Up to 33 in. in length
(about 83 cm)

Up to about 10 oz.
(about 280 g)

● Death Valley National Park, California
and Nevada
▪ Zone range

WHAT IS IT?

The SIDEWINDER or desert rattlesnake is a snake perfectly adapted to life in the driest deserts. Its long, curved, venomous fangs are located in its upper jaw.

WHAT IS THE RATTLE?

The rattle is right at the tip of its tail. It is made of coils of dry skin, which rub together and produce the rattling sound when the snake vibrates its tail.

WHERE DOES IT LIVE?

The SIDEWINDER occurs in sandy and rocky deserts with some bushes. Because of the high temperatures, it can be active only at night, except in winter.

USEFUL TO KNOW...

The SIDEWINDER bears this popular name because it progresses by throwing loops of its body to the side. Its venter scarcely touches the fine sand and the snake moves sideways.

PLAY AND LEARN!

The SIDEWINDER inflicts
its venom through...

• its tongue

• its fangs

• the tip of its tail

It inhabits only...

• the sands of Californian beaches

• prairies

• sandy and rocky deserts

It usually moves...

• forward

• backwards

• sideways

Identity Card

9.8 in.
(25 cm)

Several ounces
(several grams)

● Big Bend National Park, Texas
■ Zone range

WHAT IS IT?

The SCORPION is an arachnid just like spiders. It has a long abdomen and three pairs of legs as well as a pair of pincers. It can withstand temperatures exceeding 118°F (48°C).

HOW DOES IT HUNT?

The SCORPION is a predator that feeds on spiders, centipedes, and particularly insects, which it catches by first setting up an ambush and then poisoning them with its stinger.

HOW DOES IT KILL ITS VICTIMS?

SCORPIONS kill their prey by using the stinger at the tip of their tail to inject venom into their victim. This venom can be as strong as that of a cobra.

WHERE DOES IT LIVE?

The SCORPION lives in the undersides of rocks and underground burrows 3 ft. 3 in. (one meter) deep.

PLAY AND LEARN!

The SCORPION lives...

• under a rock

• in a burrow

• in a nest

The stinger is on its...

• pincers

• head

• tail

It feeds on...

• spiders

• mice

• seeds

THE GILA MONSTER

Identity Card

20 in.
(50 cm)

4 lbs.
(2 kg)

● Saguaro National Park, Arizona
■ Zone range

■ WHAT IS IT?

The GILA MONSTER, pronounced "HEE-luh monster," is the stoutest lizard found in the USA. It was named after the Arizona's Gila River basin, where naturalists first discovered specimens. The GILA MONSTER has a "beadwork" appearance made up of individual rounded, raised scales.

■ WHAT DOES THE GILA MONSTER EAT?

The GILA MONSTER feeds mainly on small birds, rodents, and reptile eggs. This lizard has an extremely acute sense of smell that enables it to easily locate its prey.

■ IS IT VENOMOUS?

The GILA MONSTER is one of only a handful of lizards to be venomous. First, it bites its prey and then spreads the venom. It is the only venomous lizard native to the United States.

■ DID YOU KNOW...

Like bears, GILA MONSTERS also hibernate during the winter and emerge in January or February.

PLAY AND LEARN!

The GILA MONSTER belongs to the lizard family.

• True

• False

They bite to spread their venom.

• True

• False

They hibernate during winter.

• True

• False

They have smooth skins.

• True

• False

Identity Card

Wingspan: 7.5 – 8.5 in.
(19 – 21 cm)

0.220 oz.
(10 grams)

● Grand Canyon National Park, Arizona
■ Zone range

WHAT IS IT?

It is the smallest bat that can be found in the USA. It is primarily a desert bat. It is called a CANYON BAT because of its preference for living in areas of cliffs and rocky canyons.

WHERE ARE THEIR NESTS LOCATED?

CANYON BATS usually use rock crevices for roosting sites.

WHAT IS THEIR DIET?

CANYON BATS feed on a wide variety of flying insects including beetles, moths, mosquitoes, and grasshoppers. Bats see with their ears using echolocation — they make a sound and use the echo of the sound to locate and estimate the size of something near them. Through echolocation, they not only move through the dark without bumping into trees and other obstacles, but also hunt — and hunt with precision.

DO THEY LIVE IN COLONIES?

These bats don't form large colonies like many other species. They roost singly or in very small groups.

PLAY AND LEARN!

CANYON BATS usually live...

• in a very large group

• only in couple

• in a small group

They are...

• tiny

• average size

• big

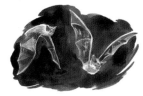

They feed on...

• flying insects

• small mammals

• seeds

THE PRONGHORN

Identity Card

3.25 – 5 ft.
(1 – 1.5 m)

90 – 150 lbs.
(41 – 68 kg)

● Grand Teton National Park, Wyoming
■ Zone range

WHAT IS IT?

The PRONGHORN is a mammal living in Western and Central North America. It closely resembles an antelope, of which it is a cousin. Some animals have horns that are more than a foot (30 cm) long and this is where their name comes from.

HOW DOES IT LIVE?

PRONGHORNS live in herds that can include up to a dozen animals. Being in groups is an adaptation for defense against predators. When they feel a threat, they run in perfect unison in a very tight, oval-shaped formation.

WHAT DO THEY EAT?

PRONGHORNS feed on a wide variety of vegetation, for example, grass or sagebrush.

HOW ARE THERE TOES?

PRONGHORNS have two long, pointed toes. They also have soft pads that allow them to walk on very hard ground.

PLAY AND LEARN!

PRONGHORNS live on their own.

• True

• False

They eat vegetation.

• True

• False

They live in eastern North America.

• True

• False

They have two distinct toes.

• True

• False

© SIMON PHIPPS - ISTOCKPHOTO

© SERGE M - FOTOLIA

© HEIKO KIERA - SHUTTERSTOCK

© BRAD THOMPSON - ISTOCKPHOTO

© FRANK LEUNG - ISTOCKPHOTO

© NICOLAS LARENTO - FOTOLIA

© J. HELGASON - SHUTTERSTOCK

© RELAXFOTO.DE - ISTOCKPHOTO

© CINDY CREIGHTON - ISTOCKPHOTO

RIVER AND LAKE ANIMALS

THE NORTH AMERICAN BEAVER

Identity Card

2 ft. 11 in. – 3 ft. 11 in. (64 – 95 cm)

From 33 to 77 lbs. (15 – 35 kg)

- Wood Buffalo National Park, Alberta and Northwest Territories (Canada)
- Zone range

WHAT IS IT?

The NORTH AMERICAN BEAVER is a rodent that has adapted itself to aquatic life. It has a slender body, big eyes, and strong paws and claws. Its thick tail measures about 5.9 inches (15 cm).

HOW DOES IT USE ITS INCISORS?

The BEAVER has very strong, sharp teeth called incisors. It is capable of bringing down trees by gnawing its way all around the tree trunk! The teeth of BEAVERS never stop growing.

WHERE DOES IT LIVE?

The BEAVER builds a lodge, made out of many sticks and mud, near the water. The lodge is protected from the exterior by a dam. The BEAVER's shelter is half-submerged in the water and the entrance is completely underwater.

WHAT IS ITS TAIL LIKE?

The BEAVER's tail is flat, hairy, and covered with scales. It uses its tail like a rudder when it is in the water.

PLAY AND LEARN!

This BEAVER uses its tail like a...

- broom
- rudder
- fin

It brings down...

- walls
- trees
- bridges

The BEAVER builds its lodge...

- in trees
- near water
- in caves

THE WOOD TURTLE

Identity Card

Up to 9.8 in.
(25 cm) in length

Up to 2.2 lbs.
(1 kg)

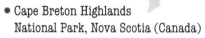

● Cape Breton Highlands
   National Park, Nova Scotia (Canada)
■ Zone range

WHAT IS IT?

The WOOD TURTLE has a beautiful, brown carapace that looks like sculpted wood. It is very difficult to spot this animal in forests or rivers because it blends in so well with its surroundings!

WHERE DOES IT LIVE?

This little turtle is an aquatic animal. It likes rivers and ponds with sandy or stony beds, but in summer, the WOOD TURTLE prefers humid undergrowth.

WHAT DOES IT EAT?

The WOOD TURTLE is extremely voracious and feeds on aquatic plants and fruit. It also consumes worms, mollusks, and fish.

USEFUL TO KNOW...

The WOOD TURTLE is a rare and endangered species, Canada. The destruction of forests presents a real threat for this little reptile.

PLAY AND LEARN!

The WOOD TURTLE lives mostly...

- in the sea

- in rivers and ponds

- in ice fields

In the summer, it can be seen...

- in burrows

- in humid undergrowth

- at the bottom of deep lakes

Its carapace is...

- sculpted and brown

- black and smooth

- yellow with a crest

THE BULLFROG

Identity Card

3.5 – 6 in.
(9 –15 cm)

1.1 lbs.
(500 grams)

● Acadia National Park, Maine
■ Zone range

■ WHAT IS IT?

The BULLFROG is one of the biggest frogs in the world — it can measure up to 17.7 in. (45 cm) with its legs extended! Its huge eardrums behind the eyes make it easy to recognize.

■ WHERE DOES IT LIVE AND WHAT DOES IT EAT?

The BULLFROG lives in lakes and ponds surrounded by dense vegetation. It is an animal with a very good appetite, and feeds on many small animals.

■ WHAT SOUND DOES IT MAKE?

The call of this frog is quite similar to the roar of a bull, which explains why it is called a BULLFROG.

■ USEFUL TO KNOW...

In the spring, the female can deposit up to 12,000 eggs in the water. The tadpoles hatch several days later but only two or three reach maturity.

PLAY AND LEARN!

This frog is called **BULLFROG** because its call is like...

• the sound of a machine

• the roar of a bull

• the sound of a plane

It lives mostly...

• in rivers and lakes

• in the grass

• in the sea

It is easily recognizable by its...

• red color

• long tail

• big eardrums

THE AMERICAN ALLIGATOR

Identity Card

 10 – 15 ft.
(3 – 4.5 m)

 1,000 lbs.
(450 kg)

● Everglades National Park, Florida
■ Zone range

PLAY AND LEARN!

WHAT IS IT?

The AMERICAN ALLIGATOR is a reptile, which means it belongs to the same zoological class as snakes and lizards. In the wild, it generally lives to be 35 to 50 years old. While in captivity, it lives longer, up to 80 years. Its skin is very hard for it is made of large, bony armored scales.

WHAT DOES THE ALLIGATOR EAT?

It likes to eat turtles, snakes, fish, birds, and small mammals.

WHERE DO THEY LIVE?

ALLIGATORS reside near freshwater rivers, lakes, and swamps. They can be found in the southeastern United States, primarily Florida and Louisiana, because of the warm environment. Despite their length and weight, they are very good swimmers thanks to their webbed feet and strong tails.

IS THE SPECIES THREATENED BY EXTINCTION?

They once faced extinction, but are no longer endangered.

AMERICAN ALLIGATORS live near lakes and swamps.

- True
- False

They are not at ease in the water.

- True
- False

They have webbed feet like ducks.

- True
- False

They have very smooth skin.

- True
- False

THE AMERICAN CROCODILE

Identity Card

Up to 15 ft.
(4.5 m)

Up to 2,000 lbs.
(910 kg)

● Biscayne National Park, Florida
■ Zone range

WHAT IS IT?

The AMERICAN CROCODILE is a reptile, and is closely related to the dinosaurs. It has a long tail, short legs, and extremely powerful jaws. Its skin is grayish-green in color and covered with scales.

HOW DOES IT BREED?

The female lays its eggs in a hole on the riverside, which she then covers with mud. The mother guards the eggs closely and is always nearby to watch over them.

HOW DOES IT BEHAVE?

The CROCODILE likes swimming and floating around in the water, with only its eyes and nostrils above the surface. This is how it discreetly observes its prey before snatching its victim, drowning it quickly and then devouring it!

WHY DOES IT CRY?

The CROCODILE cries because it has special lacrimal glands, the little organ that creates tears.

PLAY AND LEARN!

The **CROCODILE** is descended from the dinosaurs.

- True

- False

It lays its eggs in water.

- True

- False

It drowns its prey.

- True

- False

It has weak jaws.

- True

- False

THE SALMON

Identity Card

28 – 30 in.
(70 – 76 cm)

8 – 12 lbs.
(3 – 5.5 kg)

● Olympic National Park, Washington
▨ Zone range

■ WHERE DOES IT LIVE?

SALMON do not stay at the same place and in the same environment. Typically, they spend two or three years in fresh water, such as rivers or lakes. Then they start migrating to the ocean where they will spend two or three years before coming back to their native rivers to spawn (have babies). They live up to thirteen years.

■ WHAT IS ITS GREATEST NATURAL ENEMY?

Bears eat SALMON. This is the reason why bears hunt them when the SALMON leap out of the water to swim upstream.

■ ARE THEY IN DANGER?

SALMON are in danger because of human activities and climatic changes, mainly from overfishing and habitat change.

■ USEFUL TO KNOW...

SALMON is a popular food. It is considered very healthy. It is used in Japanese food to make sushi, for example.

PLAY AND LEARN!

SALMON never migrate.

- True

- False

Bears love eating SALMON.

- True

- False

Human activities don't hurt them.

- True

- False

Eating SALMON is very healthy.

- True

- False

THE RIVER OTTER

Identity Card

Up to 3 ft. 11 in. (95 cm) in length, including its tail

Up to 20.2 lbs. (9 kg)

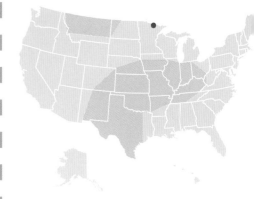

● Voyageurs National Park, Minnesota
■ Zone range

WHAT IS IT LIKE?

The RIVER OTTER is made for swimming! It has a slender body, smooth fur, powerful legs, and webbed toes.

WHERE DOES IT LIVE?

Although the RIVER OTTER is an aquatic animal, it often comes on to dry land. It lives in rivers, lakes, marshes, and estuaries. Estuaries are the watery areas on the coasts where rivers and oceans meet and mix together.

WHAT DOES IT EAT?

It is easy for the RIVER OTTER to catch fish because it is so quick. It has a very good appetite and besides eating a lot of fish, it also feeds on insects, frogs, birds, and small mammals.

USEFUL TO KNOW...

The RIVER OTTER is very playful! The mother and her babies love rolling down riverbanks into the water. However, if this mammal gets angry, it can bite hard!

PLAY AND LEARN!

The **RIVER OTTER** is a...

- fish
- reptile
- mammal

It likes...

- water
- sand
- big wheat fields

Its fur is...

- prickly
- smooth
- curly

Identity Card

Up to 14 ft.
(4.30 m) in length

Up to 800 lbs.
(360 kg)

● Voyageurs National Park, Minnesota
■ Zone range

■ WHAT IS IT?

The STURGEON is a big, dark-colored fish that is recognizable by the bony plates along the sides of its body and its pointed head ending with a specially shaped nose or snout, called a "rostrum."

■ WHERE DOES IT LIVE?

Most STURGEON live both in the sea and in rivers. It leaves the estuaries and swims up big rivers with slow currents and silt-covered riverbeds, before laying its eggs in fresh water.

■ WHAT DOES IT EAT?

It uses its rostrum and horizontal, toothless mouth to dig for worms, and small shellfish in the silt.

■ USEFUL TO KNOW...

The STURGEON is highly threatened because the females are captured before spawning. They can lay thousands of eggs, which are then made into caviar, a luxury food. The species is now protected.

PLAY AND LEARN!

The **STURGEON** is only a sea fish.

• True

• False

It has big teeth.

• True

• False

It is colorful.

• True

• False

It produces caviar.

• True

• False

THE FLORIDA MANATEE

Identity Card

Up to 15 ft. 91 in.
(4.85 meters) in length

Up to 3,400 lbs.
(1,550 kg)

• Canaveral National Seashore, Florida
* Zone range

WHERE DOES IT LIVE?

The MANATEE is a big mammal with a fish-shaped body. It is slow and calm and lives in the warm, shallow waters of estuaries, and in the marshy coastlines in America.

IS IT AN ENDANGERED SPECIES?

The MANATEE has been hunted for its meat and also just for pleasure. Nowadays, it suffers greatly from the development of tourism along the coast, which destroys its natural habitat. Many manatees are injured by yacht propellers.

HOW CAN IT BE PRESERVED?

The only way to save the MANATEE and prevent it from being killed is to preserve the vast coastal regions and educate the public so that this animal can live in peace. It is seriously endangered.

USEFUL TO KNOW...

Given its size and its habit of grazing on seaweed and sea grass, it has been nicknamed the "sea cow." It is a very calm animal that loves playing with divers.

PLAY AND LEARN!

The MANATEE is a...

• fish

• reptile

• mammal

It lives in...

• freezing waters

• warm coastal waters

• the depths of oceans

It feeds on...

• fish

• seaweed and sea grass

• shrimp

© PAUL TESSIER - ISTOCKPHOTO

© MATTJEPPSON - FOTOLIA

© JEAN-PAUL DEMOLIN - FOTOLIA

© FRANK PARKER - ISTOCKPHOTO

© ANNA YU - ISTOCKPHOTO

© FRANK LEUNG - ISTOCKPHOTO

© KAPHOTO - FOTOLIA

© KOJIHIRANO - ISTOCKPHOTO

© RÈMY GUERRIER - FOTOLIA

MOUNTAIN ANIMALS

THE BIGHORN SHEEP

Identity Card

 5 – 6 ft.
(150 – 180 cm)

117 – 279 lbs.
(50 – 130 kg)

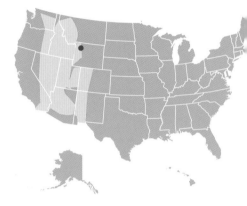

- Yellowstone National Park, Wyoming, Montana and Idaho
- Zone range

WHAT IS IT?

The BIGHORN SHEEP is a species of sheep in North America named for its large horns. These impressive growths are a weapon used in battles and a symbol of status. Males fight for dominance. Their fights can easily last more than 24 hours.

WHAT DOES IT EAT?

It follows a different diet according to the season. During winter, it will eat woody plants such as willow and sage. During spring and summer, however, it prefers grass, seeds, and plants.

IS THIS SPECIES THREATENED?

This species is threatened with eventual extinction. Their main threats are unregulated or illegal hunting, diseases, competition from livestock, and human presence on their habitat.

USEFUL TO KNOW...

They live in a large group called a "herd." A female herd has about 5 to 15 ewes (females) and their babies; male groups, only 2 to 5. In the winter, the males and females get together.

PLAY AND LEARN!

BIGHORN SHEEPS never use their horns.

- True
- False

Males live in a smaller group than ew

- True
- False

Their fights can last more than 24 hour

- True
- False

The species is threatened.

- True
- False

THE GRIZZLY BEAR

Identity Card

Up to 9 feet 2 in.
(2.80 m)

1,322 lbs.
(600 kg)

- Yellowstone National Park, Wyoming, Montana and Idaho
- Zone range

WHAT IS IT?

The GRIZZLY BEAR is a kind of bear from the North American continent. Despite its imposing body, it is an agile creature and can stand up on its two hind legs.

HOW DOES IT HUNT?

The GRIZZLY BEAR hunts at night and makes the most of its keen sense of smell to find its food. It uses its long-clawed forelegs to attack moose, caribou, Rocky Mountain goats, and deer. This bear also eats plants, fish, honey, and many little animals.

HOW DOES IT BEHAVE?

The GRIZZLY BEAR is a solitary animal. It loves water and spends a lot of time in rivers, which are rich in salmon.

WHAT DOES IT DO IN THE WINTER?

In the fall, it eats a lot to build up sufficient fat reserves to survive during the long hibernation period when it retreats into its den and sleeps.

PLAY AND LEARN!

The **GRIZZLY BEAR can stand up straight on...**

- its hind legs
- its forelegs
- its back

It loves...

- prairies
- water
- rocks

It hunts with...

- its hooves
- its claws
- its mouth

Identity Card

23.5 in.
(60 cm)

7 lbs.
(3 kg)

● Voyageurs National Park, Minnesota
■ Zone range

WHAT IS IT?

The GROUNDHOG is a rodent. It is a small mammal with a brown coat, a long black tail measuring 6.3 inches (16 cm), and very big, sharp teeth.

WHAT IS ITS DEN LIKE?

In the spring, the GROUNDHOG makes a den more than 33 feet (10 m) long and about 10 feet (3 m) deep. It hibernates in the winter for at least eight months.

HOW DOES IT SURVIVE?

The GROUNDHOG eats grass, seeds, and roots. During the hibernation period, its heartbeat slows down to just four beats a minute, during which time it breathes only once.

USEFUL TO KNOW...

In the summer, the GROUNDHOG usually lives alone. It constantly watches over its territory and its excellent sense of hearing warns it of the presence of any predators.

PLAY AND LEARN!

The GROUNDHOG goes...

- into retirement

- on vacation

- into hibernation

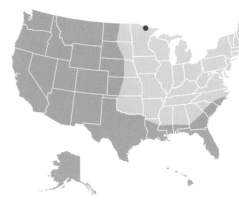

It eats...

- birds

- fish

- grass

Its den is...

- deep

- shallow

- open

Identity Card

 Up to 7 ft. 10 in. (2.40 m) in length, including the tail

66 lbs. – 265 lbs. (30 – 120 kg)

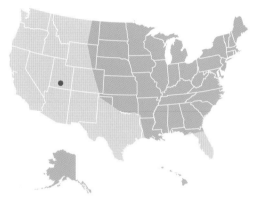

● Bryce Canyon National Park, Utah
■ Zone range

WHERE DOES IT LIVE?

The COUGAR is a big, solitary mammal with a slender and agile body. It is also known as a "mountain lion" or "puma."

HOW DOES IT HUNT?

The COUGAR is both nimble and alert and it lies low among the rocks to observe its prey. In winter, once it has captured and killed its prey, the COUGAR hides it under the snow.

WHAT DOES IT LOOK LIKE?

The COUGAR has a short, reddish-brown or yellowish coat. Its underbody and chin is white and its muzzle is black and white. It also has a long tail measuring 3 ft. 3 in. (1 m).

HOW LARGE IS ITS TERRITORY?

Males and females have separate territories. The males occupy a territory of about 108 square miles (about 280 km²) that often overlaps into the area of the females, which measures about 55 square miles (about 140 km²).

PLAY AND LEARN!

The COUGAR is also called a "puma."

• True

• False

Its coat is short.

• True

• False

It hides its prey under the snow.

• True

• False

It has a long tail.

• True

• False

THE BLACK BEAR

Identity Card

6 ft. 6 in.
(up to 2 meters) in length

About 615 lbs.
(about 280 kg)

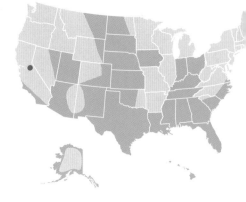

● Yosemite National Park, California
■ Zone range

PLAY AND LEARN!

WHAT IS IT?

The BLACK BEAR is smaller than its cousin, the grizzly bear. It has thick fur, which is often black but it can also be light brown or beige. Its pointed muzzle is brown and its paws have very strong claws. This bear is capable of standing up on its hind legs.

WHERE DOES IT LIVE AND WHAT DOES IT EAT?

The BLACK BEAR lives in dense forests on the plains and in rocky mountainous areas and mostly eats plants. This bear leads a solitary life.

WHAT DOES IT DO IN THE WINTER?

The BLACK BEAR retreats into its den during the whole winter period. However, it does not hibernate; it remains dormant and survives on its own body's fat reserves.

USEFUL TO KNOW...

The BLACK BEAR is quite common and is protected by laws. The average lifespan of this bear is 30 years.

The BLACK BEAR mostly eats plants.

• True

• False

It lives in the desert.

• True

• False

This bear lives in a group.

• True

• False

It hunts in the winter.

• True

• False

THE MOUNTAIN KINGSNAKE

Identity Card

20 – 48 in.
(50 to 122 cm) in length

Up to 4.5 oz.
(about 130 grams)

- Yosemite National Park, California
- Zone range

WHAT IS IT?

The MOUNTAIN KINGSNAKE is a small snake, one of the many harmless snakes. Its body is stiff and muscular. Its short, stout head is well adapted to its life in forest litter.

WHAT DOES IT EAT?

The MOUNTAIN KINGSNAKE eats small lizards that it finds in their shelters, as well as other small snakes. It is also fond of nestling rodents.

WHERE DOES IT LIVE?

The MOUNTAIN KINGSNAKE is a typical inhabitant of moist fir forests and wooded canyons. It is usually associated with rocky areas, in which this secretive snake finds a lot of shelters.

USEFUL TO KNOW...

This red, black and white snake is often called a "coral snake." However, it is totally harmless, in contrast to true coral snakes that are dangerously venomous.

PLAY AND LEARN!

The **MOUNTAIN KINGSNAKE** is found in the warmest deserts.

- True
- False

It eats mainly lizards.

- True
- False

It is a dangerous "coral snake."

- True
- False

It is often found among rocks.

- True

- False

THE CALIFORNIA CONDOR

Identity Card

Wingspan: 9 – 10 ft.
(2.7 – 3 m)

Up to 30 lbs.
(13.5 kg)

● Grand Canyon National Park, Arizona
■ Zone range

PLAY AND LEARN!

WHAT IS IT?

The CALIFORNIA CONDOR is a bird of prey belonging to the vulture family. It is easily recognizable by its black and white plumage and its bald head. Its immense wings make it one of the biggest birds alive.

WHERE DOES IT LIVE?

CALIFORNIA CONDORS live in northern Arizona, southern Utah and coastal California. They are often found near cliffs or large trees, which they use as nesting sites. Today, about 130 birds live in the wild.

WHAT DOES IT EAT?

It is a carrion eater feeding on the decaying flesh of dead animals. It can also attack injured animals.

USEFUL TO KNOW...

The CALIFORNIA CONDOR has a cousin in South America, in the mountainous region as suggested by its name, the Andean condor.

The CALIFORNIA CONDOR is a bird of prey.

• True

• False

It lives in the mountains.

• True

• False

It lives in Europe.

• True

• False

It feeds mainly on dead animals.

• True

• False

THE WILD TURKEY

Identity Card

39 – 49 in.
(1 – 1.25 m)

11 – 24 lbs.
(5 – 11 kg)

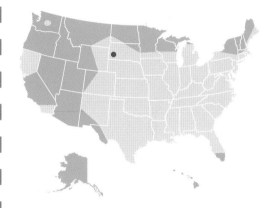

● Wind Cave National Park, South Dakota
▪ Zone range

WHAT IS IT?

The WILD TURKEY is very noticeable with its black or white feathers, large fan-shaped tail, and bald neck, as well as the red wattle hanging from its neck. Despite its weight, it is an agile flyer, unlike its cousin, the domesticated turkey. It also gobbles.

WHAT DOES IT EAT?

The WILD TURKEY spends time searching for food on forest floors. They feed on nuts, seeds, fruits, insects, and salamanders.

WHAT DOES IT PRODUCE?

Turkey is the traditional Thanksgiving meal and its meat is excellent. Although they are edible, turkey eggs are not eaten because farmers keep them to raise poults (baby turkeys).

USEFUL TO KNOW...

WILD TURKEY reintroduction programs began in the 1940s. The birds were relocated to areas where turkey populations had been decimated. The program worked so well that wild turkeys now live in areas where they had never been found before.

PLAY AND LEARN!

The WILD TURKEY quacks.

- True
- False

It lives in water.

- True
- False

The WILD TURKEY searches for food in farmyards.

- True
- False

It is mostly eaten at Easter.

- True
- False

THE RED FOX

Identity Card

 About 3 ft. 3 in. (1 m)

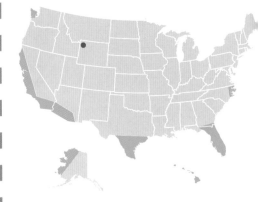 8.8 – 15.4 lbs. (4 – 7 kg)

- Yellowstone National Park, Wyoming, Montana and Idaho
- Zone range

■ WHAT IS IT?
The RED FOX is a very quick, agile mammal belonging to the dog family. It has a pointed muzzle, a thick coat, big ears, and a long tail, which can measure up to 17.7 in. (45 cm).

■ WHERE DOES IT LIVE?
The RED FOX lives in the forest but adapts very well to all types of environments and will even venture to the outskirts of cities in search of food.

■ WHAT IS ITS COAT LIKE?
The RED FOX has thick, shaggy fur and its color varies from gray to reddish-brown, which is the most common. Its chin, throat, and the front of its chest are white.

■ WHAT DOES IT EAT?
Small mammals, birds, eggs, fish, and berries make up the RED FOX's regular diet. Sometimes, it does eat chickens!

PLAY AND LEARN!

Where does the FOX live?

- In the forest
- In the savannah
- In the sea

It eats...

- chickens
- grass
- pineapple

Its coat is...

- red
- yellow
- spotted

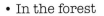

Identity Card

About 2 ft. 3 in. (70 cm) – 5 ft. 10 in. (1.5 m) including wingspan

3.3 – 9.3 lbs. (1.5 – 4.2 kg)

● Grand Teton National Park, Wyoming
■ Zone range

WHAT IS IT?

The GREAT HORNED OWL is a bird of prey with a short and stocky body. It is recognizable by the two tufts of brown-black feathers on its head, its big orange eyes, and pale, creamy gray or reddish plumage.

DOES IT HAVE GOOD VISION?

The GREAT HORNED OWL has a very wide range of vision because it can turn its head around without moving the rest of its body. It also sees very well at night.

WHEN AND WHAT DOES IT HUNT?

The GREAT HORNED OWL always hunts at night. It is a skillful predator that flies low to seize its prey, which includes little mammals and birds. Sometimes, this big bird even attacks foxes!

WHY DOES IT SCARE US?

The eerie calls of OWLS can be a little scary at night but these beautiful birds are harmless.

PLAY AND LEARN!

The GREAT HORNED OWL has a...

- long body

- thin body

- short and stocky body

It feeds on...

- fish

- mammals

- fruits

On its head, it has...

- two horns

- two tufts of feathers

- two ears

© ALONBOU - FOTOLIA

Identity Card

15 – 18.9 in.
(38 – 48 cm) in length

18.8 – 56.5 oz.
(530 – 1,600 grams)

● Shenandoah National Park, Virginia
■ Zone range

WHAT IS IT?

When the PEREGRINE FALCON soars up into the sky, folds back its wings and dives at high speed, it is the fastest bird in the world! This falcon is famous for these spectacular dives, called "stoops."

WHERE DOES IT LIVE?

The PEREGRINE FALCON lives on a cliff, often under a rocky overhang that protects it from the rain. This bird does not build nests. It mates for life.

WHAT ARE BABY FALCONS LIKE?

When they hatch, the chicks have a pretty white down but it is too fine to protect them from the cold so they stay huddled together under their mother's feathers.

USEFUL TO KNOW...

The PEREGRINE FALCON's incredible vision enables it to detect its prey (mostly only birds) up to a mile away!

PLAY AND LEARN!

The **PEREGRINE FALCON** has...

- excellent vision
- excellent hearing
- excellent sense of smell

It lives in...

- Antarctica
- North America
- Asia

Its chicks are born with...

- a white down
- a gray tail
- yellowish beak

© RICK PARSONS – SHUTTERSTOCK

© WIREPEC – FOTOLIA

© MENNO SCHAEFER – SHUTTERSTOCK

© MARY STEPHENS – ISTOCKPHOTO

© SEBASTIAN SANTA – ISTOCKPHOTO

© FRED KAMPHUES – SHUTTERSTOCK

© JU-LEE – ISTOCKPHOTO

© LEN TILLIM – ISTOCKPHOTO

© DANIEL LESNIAK – FOTOLIA

PRAIRIE ANIMALS

THE BOBCAT

Identity Card

26 – 42 in.
(66 – 110 cm)

11 – 30 lbs.
(5 – 14 kg)

● Yosemite National Park, California
■ Zone range

PLAY AND LEARN!

BOBCATS are...

- good hunters

- big sleepers

- gourmets

They have...

- round ears

- pointy ears

- dangling ears

It is the cousin of...

- cat

- fox

- lynx

WHAT IS IT?

The BOBCAT is a wild cat and is the cousin of the lynx; both have little black tufts at the tips of their ears. BOBCATS are the most common wildcats on the North American continent.

HOW IS THEIR FUR?

The BOBCAT's coat is light brown to reddish. Its fur is covered in black spots that fade into light black streaks.

ARE THEY HUNTERS?

BOBCATS are fierce hunters and can hunt a prey bigger than them. Their diet includes rabbits, mice, and squirrels. Generally, they hunt at night because that is when their prey come out.

WHERE DO THEY LIVE?

BOBCATS have a territory of about 100 square miles. Female bobcats have their own territory that overlaps the males' territory.

Identity Card

22 – 54 in.
(55 – 140 cm)

5.3 oz.
(150 grams)

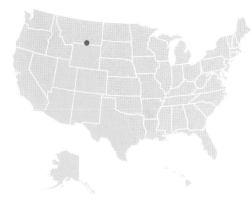

- Bighorn National Recreation Area, Montana and Wyoming
- Zone range

WHAT IS IT?

The COMMON GARTER SNAKE is a small snake, which belongs to the family of aquatic grass snakes and is recognizable by its yellow and black stripes. Its skin is soft and not at all slimy.

WHERE DOES IT LIVE?

This snake lives in humid places such as prairies, forests, riversides, and near ponds. It hides in the grass and bushes.

HOW DOES IT LIVE AND WHAT DOES IT EAT?

The COMMON GARTER SNAKE likes basking in the sun and often goes swimming. It feeds mainly on frogs and fish. It does not lay eggs but instead gives birth to baby snakes.

USEFUL TO KNOW...

It is a very common, harmless snake, which can be found near small towns. It is not aggressive unless it feels threatened.

PLAY AND LEARN!

The COMMON GARTER SNAKE is venomous.

- True
- False

It eats frogs.

- True
- False

It lives in the desert.

- True
- False

It lays eggs.

- True
- False

THE SMOOTH GREEN SNAKE

Identity Card

11 – 26 in.
(28 – 66 cm)

Up to 0.35 oz.
(20 grams)

● Bryce Canyon National Park, Utah
▪ Zone range

■ WHAT IS IT?

The name of the SMOOTH GREEN SNAKE suits it well because it is as green as the grass! This snake is small, slender, and supple with smooth and silky scales.

■ WHY IS IT GREEN?

The SMOOTH GREEN SNAKE lives in the grass and thickets where it can easily blend into the green vegetation that matches its color. This snake is a master of camouflage!

■ HOW DOES IT LIVE AND WHAT DOES IT EAT?

The SMOOTH GREEN SNAKE likes the sun but is rarely visible. It prefers to hide in the grass and observe its prey, which include insects, caterpillars, and spiders. This snake lays small, white eggs.

■ USEFUL TO KNOW...

The SMOOTH GREEN SNAKE is no doubt the most elegant of all the snakes in North America. It is completely harmless.

PLAY AND LEARN!

The SMOOTH GREEN SNAKE has silky scales.

- True

- False

It lives mostly in burrows.

- True

- False

It hunts lizards.

- True

- False

It is a good climber.

- True

- False

Identity Card

 Up to 9.8 in. (25 cm) in length

Up to 0.71 oz. (20 grams)

● Bryce Canyon National Park, Utah
▪ Zone range

■ WHAT IS IT?

The SPOTTED SALAMANDER is easy to recognize with its big, plump, black body and colorful yellow or orange blotches!

■ CAN IT MOVE FAST?

The SPOTTED SALAMANDER has very short legs. It moves very slowly, just like any other salamander. The adult is not a good swimmer.

■ WHERE AND HOW DOES IT LIVE?

The SPOTTED SALAMANDER lives in the litter of very damp forests and in the vegetation around ponds. It is a discreet animal and comes out at night or during heavy downpours to capture insects and worms.

■ USEFUL TO KNOW...

The SPOTTED SALAMANDER is a common animal but very shy. It looks like a lizard but because it is an amphibian, there are no scales on its body.

PLAY AND LEARN!

The **SPOTTED SALAMANDER**'s body is covered in...

- feathers
- hair
- scale

It is always in...

- sand
- water
- grass

It has spots on its...

- whole body
- head
- tail

THE PRAIRIE DOG

Identity Card

12 – 15 in.
(30 – 40 cm)

2 – 4 lbs.
(1 – 2 kg)

● Theodore Roosevelt National Park, North Da
■ Zone range

PLAY AND LEARN!

WHAT ARE THEY?

PRAIRIE DOGS are rodents living in the prairies and open grasslands. They are named after their habitat and warning call, which sounds similar to a dog's bark.

WHERE DO THEY LIVE?

PRAIRIE DOGS dig their burrows underground and mainly live at altitudes ranging from 2,000 to 10,000 ft. above sea level. Their underground burrows become a real protection against very high temperatures in summer and very cold temperatures in the winter.

DO THEY LIVE IN A COMMUNITY?

PRAIRIE DOGS are very social and like to live in large colonies or "towns." One colony can count more than a thousand prairie dogs. Each colony is then divided into neighborhoods.

WHAT IS THEIR DISTINCTIVE FEATURE?

PRAIRIE DOGS like to greet each other by touching their noses and moving their heads sideways.

They like to live on their own.

- True

- False

Their burrows are underground to protect themselves.

- True

- False

They live at altitudes up to 10,000 fee

- True

- False

Their call sounds like a barking dog.

- True

- False

THE AMERICAN BISON

Identity Card

About 11 ft. 5 in. (3.5 m) in length

Up to 2,500 lbs. (1,130 kg)

● Grand Teton National Park, Wyoming
■ Zone range

WHAT IS IT?

The AMERICAN BISON is a cousin of the cow. With its long shaggy coat, enormous head, and muscular chest, it is a very impressive mammal.

HOW DOES IT LIVE?

In the past, AMERICAN BISON lived in huge herds of hundreds of thousands of animals. It only eats grass.

WHERE DOES IT LIVE?

AMERICAN BISON used to travel across the Great Plains in North America. Nowadays, AMERICAN BISON live on preserves and on ranches.

IS IT AN ENDANGERED SPECIES?

The AMERICAN BISON became nearly extinct at the end of the 19th century because settlers hunted them in great numbers for their meat. There are now about 40,000 animals living in the wild.

PLAY AND LEARN!

AMERICAN BISON are cousins of the...

- whale
- cow
- monkey

They live in vast...

- rivers
- forests
- prairies

They always...

- live in a couple
- live on their own
- live in a herd

THE BLACK-FOOTED FERRET

Identity Card

Up to 15.7 in.
(40 cm)

1.5 – 2.5 lbs.
(0.700 – 1.2 kg)

● Badlands National Park, South Dakota
■ Zone range

WHAT IS IT?

The FERRET is the domesticated form of the polecat. It is carnivorous and has a long, slender body, a bushy tail, short legs, a pointed nose, and light-colored fur.

IS IT DANGEROUS?

The FERRET can be trained like a cat but it has to be taught not to bite its master. It is an intelligent animal and quickly adapts to living in a house but... it does have a strong smell!

HOW DOES IT BEHAVE AND WHAT DOES IT EAT?

The FERRET is an inquisitive creature and full of life! It loves playing but sleeps at least 16 hours a day. As it is carnivorous, it feeds on small animals, but it can eat special ferret food.

USEFUL TO KNOW...

The FERRET was domesticated over 2,500 years ago. The Greeks, Romans and our ancestors in the Middle Ages kept ferrets as pets. Its average lifespan is 10 years.

PLAY AND LEARN!

The FERRET is carnivorous.

• True

• False

It sleeps a lot.

• True

• False

It is very playful.

• True

• False

It is bigger than a hamster.

• True

• False

THE BADGER

Identity Card

35 in. (tail included)
(90 cm)

20 – 24 lbs.
(9 – 11 kg)

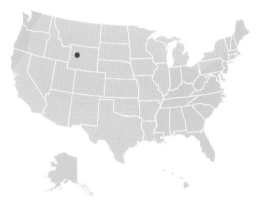

● Grand Teton National Park, Wyoming
■ Zone range

WHAT IS IT?

BADGERS have black faces with distinctive white markings, gray bodies with a white stripe from head to tail, and dark legs with light-colored stomachs. They have rather short, fat bodies, with short legs built for digging.

WHAT IS THEIR DIET?

BADGERS like to eat earthworms, insects, grubs, reptiles, birds, fruits, and roots.

HOW ARE THEIR BURROWS?

The burrows and dens of BADGERS are extremely important to their lifestyle. They use them for hunting, sleeping, storing food, and giving birth. Their den has only one entrance.

USEFUL TO KNOW...

BADGERS can run up to 16 – 19 mph for short periods. They are able to fight with much larger animals, such as wolves or bears. They can be fierce animals and are never afraid of protecting themselves.

PLAY AND LEARN!

BADGERS eat ...

- fish

- grass

- earthworms

How many entrances does its burrow have?

- More than 10

- Between two or three

- Only one

What color is the stripe on its back?

- White

- Gray

- Red

THE LEST WEASEL

Identity Card

6.5 – 8 in.
(16.5 – 20 cm)

1 – 2 oz.
(30 – 60 grams)

● Voyageurs National Park, Minnesota
■ Zone range

WHAT IS IT?

LEAST WEASELS are long and slender, with a long neck, a narrow head, and short limbs. They have large, black eyes and large, round ears.

HOW DO THEY COMMUNICATE WITH EACH OTHER?

LEAST WEASELS have a strong sense of smell. They use it to sense their prey but also to communicate with each other. They also have different vocalizations to warn the herd of close predators.

WHERE CAN WE FOUND THEM?

They can be found on every continent except Antartica. They can adapt to open forests, farmlands, meadows, prairies, and steppes.

WHAT IS THEIR DIET?

LEAST WEASELS feed mostly on small rodents, such as mice and hamsters. Despite its small size, the least weasel is a fierce hunter, capable of catching rabbits.

PLAY AND LEARN!

LEAST WEASELS are found only...

• in Europe

• in America

• everywhere in the world

They feed on...

• small rodents

• seeds

• grass and insects

They live in...

• water

• prairies

• mountains

SEA ANIMALS

THE BLUE WHALE

WHAT IS IT?

Although it has a tail like a fish and big fins, the BLUE WHALE is not a fish; it is a mammal. It is the biggest animal on Earth. Its thick layer of whale blubber enables it to withstand freezing cold temperatures.

WHERE AND HOW DOES IT LIVE?

The BLUE WHALE can be mostly found in cold or very cold waters. It often comes up to the surface to breathe by a hole behind its head, which is called the blowhole or the spout.

WHAT DOES IT EAT?

The BLUE WHALE has a huge mouth but no real teeth. It captures shrimps with its big baleen plates and devours between three to four tons of plankton per day.

USEFUL TO KNOW...

The BLUE WHALE is more gray than blue. Whales can produce loud sounds called the "whale song." They are becoming extinct.

PLAY AND LEARN!

The BLUE WHALE is a...

• mammal

• fish

• rodent

It lives in...

• warm waters

• cold waters

• lakes

It makes...

• a call

• sounds

• a roar

Identity Card

 Up to 62 ft. 4 in. in length (19 m)

Up to 38 tons

● Glacier Bay National Park & Preserve, Alaska
▨ Zone range

■ WHAT IS IT?

The HUMPBACK WHALE has a black back, very long flippers similar in shape to the wings of a plane, and a head covered with small nodules.

■ HOW DOES IT LIVE?

In the summer, the HUMPBACK WHALE prefers cold waters; in the winter, it goes to tropical waters where it breeds. It can cover distances of up to 15,000 miles (25,000 km) a year!

■ IS IT AGILE?

Despite its great mass, the HUMPBACK WHALE can make spectacular jumps out of the water. When it falls heavily back into the sea, it creates an enormous splash!

■ USEFUL TO KNOW...

Although the HUMPBACK WHALE has a triangular tail and big flippers, it is not a fish. It is a marine mammal. This whale's "song" is both powerful and complex.

PLAY AND LEARN!

The HUMPBACK WHALE is white.

• True

• False

It likes to jump like an acrobat.

• True

• False

It is a fish.

• True

• False

It has big wings.

• True

• False

THE HARBOR SEAL

Identity Card

 Up to 5 ft. 10 in. (1.50 m) in length

Up to 265 lbs. (120 kg)

● Kenai Fjord National Park, Alaska
▨ Zone range

■ WHAT IS IT?

The HARBOR SEAL is a sea mammal with a gray, slender body. When on land, it hauls itself along on its tummy but in the water, it swims as well as a fish! It uses its short, wide feet like flippers.

■ WHERE DOES IT LIVE?

The HARBOR SEAL lives on seashores. At low tide, it can be seen resting on sandbanks but at high tide, it goes swimming and diving.

■ IS IT A SOCIABLE CREATURE?

HARBOR SEALS live in huge colonies. Young seals, or pups, are very playful but the seal can also be aggressive!

■ USEFUL TO KNOW...

The HARBOR SEAL is protected from the cold by a thick layer of fat. This species is seriously endangered because of hunting and coastal development.

PLAY AND LEARN!

HARBOR SEALS live mostly in warm waters.

- True
- False

It is friendly.

- True
- False

It runs fast.

- True
- False

It is an endangered species.

- True

- False

Identity Card

 Up to 3 ft. 3 in. (1 m) in length

Up to 1.1 lbs. (500 g)

- Acadia National Park, Maine
- Zone range

WHAT IS IT?

The ATLANTIC LOBSTER is a big ocean crustacean (an animal with a hard outer shell and several pairs of legs). It has two big pincers, ten legs, and a tough, black and orange carapace to protect its body. It also has a strong tail.

HOW DOES IT SWIM?

The ATLANTIC LOBSTER swims backwards by moving its tail around but it uses only its legs when it moves along the ocean bed.

WHERE DOES IT LIVE?

The ATLANTIC LOBSTER lives near rocky coastlines, in cold and deep ocean waters. It hides under the rocks or in a hole in the sand. It never leaves the water.

USEFUL TO KNOW...

Lobsters are fished in great quantities because their delicious flesh is very popular. Consequently, this species is becoming rare.

PLAY AND LEARN!

The ATLANTIC LOBSTER is a...

- fish
- crustacean
- mollusk

It lives mostly...

- on sandy beaches
- in the ocean among the rocks
- in the mud

It is easily recognizable by its...

- red fins
- yellow shell
- black and orange carapace

THE GREAT WHITE SHARK

© CDELACY - FOTOLIA

Identity Card

Up to 21 ft.
(6.4 m) in length

Up to 7,000 lbs.
(3,175 kg)

● Channel Islands National Park, California
※ Zone range

WHAT IS IT?

The GREAT WHITE SHARK is surely one of the greatest living predatory fish. The jaws of its wide mouth are fitted out with strong, sharp teeth. The triangular shape of its large dorsal fin is typical of sharks.

WHERE DOES IT LIVE?

It mostly inhabits shallow waters along the coasts of temperate seas and oceans. It is not fond of warm waters. This shark lives on its own.

ON WHAT DOES IT PREY?

Its appetite seems to be endless! The GREAT WHITE SHARK may attack any kind of marine animal passing close to its jaws but it mainly preys upon seals.

USEFUL TO KNOW...

The GREAT WHITE SHARK can attack humans but it is not a blood-thirsty monster. Most attacks occur in shallow waters.

PLAY AND LEARN!

The **GREAT WHITE SHARK is...**

- a fish
- a mammal
- a marine reptile

It eats mainly...

- algae
- shrimps
- seals

It inhabits mainly:

- the bottom of oceans
- large rivers
- coastal waters

Identity Card

Up to 19 ft. 6 in. (6 m)

Up to 8,500 lbs. (3,850 kg)

● Point Reyes National Seashore, California

▨ Zone range

WHAT IS IT?

The ELEPHANT SEAL is a mammal and the male has a large, heavy body, a big, short nose, and a gray coat.

HOW DOES IT DEFEND ITSELF?

The ELEPHANT SEAL threatens opponents by curving its back into a "U" shape to intimidate other males and ensure its dominance over the group.

HOW FAR CAN IT DIVE?

The ELEPHANT SEAL can dive up to 330 feet (about 100 meters) deep in freezing waters, where it goes fishing for skate, cuttlefish, and shellfish.

DOES ITS NOSE INFLATE?

The ELEPHANT SEAL uses its nose to make loud noises but the nose does not inflate, unlike other species such as the hooded seal.

PLAY AND LEARN!

The ELEPHANT SEAL can dive down to...

• 328 feet (100 m)

• 65 feet 7 inches (20 m)

• 984 feet 3 inches (300 m)

Its nose is...

• long

• short

• thin

When it threatens, it curves...

• its mouth

• its back

• its flippers

THE STELLER SEA LION

Identity Card

males: about 10 – 11 ft. (3 – 3.5 m)
females: about 7.5 – 9.5 ft. (2.3 – 2.9 m)

males: up to 2,500 lbs. (1,130 kg)
females: up to 770 lbs. (350 kg)

● Channel Islands National Park, California
● Zone range

PLAY AND LEARN!

■ WHAT IS IT?

The STELLER SEA LION is the largest member of the seal family. It is named after Georg Wilhelm Steller, the naturalist who first described them in the 18th century.

■ WHAT ARE THEIR DIETS?

STELLER SEA LIONS mainly hunt a wide variety of fish, such as cod, salmon, or squid. Their diet may vary seasonally. They may range far and wide to find their prey, but are not known to migrate.

■ IS THE STELLER SEA LION IN DANGER?

Since 1990, the STELLER SEA LION is listed as an endangered species. Its population declined steadily for about 30 years.

■ USEFUL TO KNOW...

STELLER SEA LIONS are very social. They like to gather throughout the year. At sea, they are seen alone or in small groups, but they will periodically get together on land in large groups called "rookeries" or "haul outs."

STELLER SEA LIONS migrate.

• True

• False

They were named after the sound they make, like the lion's roaring.

• True

• False

They are the largest of their species.

• True

• False

They mainly feed on fish.

• True

• False

THE SWORDFISH

Identity Card

From 9.8 ft. (3 m) in length

90 – 200 pounds (40 – 90 kg)

● Padre Island National Seashore, Texas

▨ Zone range

WHAT IS IT?

The SWORDFISH is a highly migratory fish that is recognizable by its long and flat bill. They are one of the fastest species in the ocean thanks to their slim body, swimming up to 50 mph.

WHY DO THEY MIGRATE?

The SWORDFISH migrates in warmer waters in winter and cooler waters in summer. When they are in deep parts of the ocean, a special organ warms up their brain and their eyes.

HOW LONG DO THEY LIVE?

The SWORDFISH can live up to nine years. It is said they have reached maturity at the age of four or five years.

USEFUL TO KNOW...

The SWORDFISH is called after its bill that looks like a sword. The fish uses it to slash at its prey such as mackerel, menhaden, bluefish, or squids. They feed on the surface at night.

PLAY AND LEARN!

The SWORDFISH lives in...

- rivers
- warm waters
- arctic waters

It uses its bill to...

- swim faster
- hunt fish
- feel the heat

It can live up to...

- four years
- seven years
- nine years

THE GRAY WHALE

Identity Card

 40 – 50 ft.
(12 – 15 m)

 30 – 40 tons

● Olympic National Park, Washington
▧ Zone range

WHAT IS IT?

The GRAY WHALE has no teeth. It uses its snout to forage by dislodging tiny creatures from the seafloor. It then filters these morsels with its baleen. It also has two blowholes on top of its head, which can create a distinctive V-shaped blow.

ARE THEY MIGRATORS?

GRAY WHALES are great migrators. They travel in large groups, called pods. They swim up to 12,500 miles, moving from the cold Alaskan water to the warmer streams of the Mexican coasts.

WHY IS IT CALLED "GRAY WHALE"?

The common name of the GRAY WHALE comes from the gray patches and white mottling on its dark skin left by parasites.

WHICH OTHER ANIMAL IS FEARED BY THE GRAY WHALE?

The only non-human predators of the GRAY WHALE are killer whales.

PLAY AND LEARN!

GRAY WHALES have huge teeth.

• True

• False

They stay all year long in the same area

• True

• False

They are scared of killer whales.

• True

• False

They feed on tiny creatures found on the sea floor.

• True

• False

Identity Card

 Up to 26 ft. 2 in. (8 m) wide

From 1.2 to 3 tons

- Virgin Islands National Park, Virgin Islands
  Zone range

WHAT IS IT?

The MANTA RAY is the biggest of all rays. Like sharks, its skeleton is formed of cartilage instead of bones. Its eyes are on the upper side of its body and its mouth is underneath.

WHERE DOES IT LIVE?

The MANTA RAY lives in the warm waters of the Atlantic, Indian, and Pacific Oceans. It hunts other fish near the water's surface and often makes impressive leaps out of the water.

HOW DOES IT SWIM?

This RAY's big fins are as long as its body and it uses them like wings to advance in the water. Its tail acts as a rudder.

USEFUL TO KNOW...

The MANTA RAY is also called "the sea devil" but it is totally harmless.

PLAY AND LEARN!

The MANTA RAY has...

- big bones

- thick cartilage

- no skeleton

It lives in...

- rivers

- cold waters

- warm waters

It lives...

- at the bottom of the ocean

- at the surface of the ocean

- near beaches

THE LEATHERBACK SEA TURTLE

© STEPHANIE ROUSSEAU - SHUTTERSTOCK

Identity Card

Up to 8 ft.
(2.45 m)

Up to 2,000 lbs.
(900 kg)

● Biscayne National Park, Florida
▨ Zone range

WHAT IS IT?

The LEATHERBACK SEA TURTLE is a marine turtle. Its carapace, or shell, is the largest of all living turtles. However, instead of being hard, like other sea turtles, it is covered with a thick, leathery skin. In place of feet, it has large and powerful flippers.

WHAT DOES IT EAT?

The LEATHERBACK SEA TURTLE feeds on small squid, crabs, and, in particular, a large quantity of jellyfish. The venom of jellyfish does not harm this turtle.

WHERE DOES IT LIVE?

It lives in all of the oceans, far out at sea as well as near the coasts. It lays its eggs on certain beaches in the tropics.

USEFUL TO KNOW...

The LEATHERBACK SEA TURTLE is a greatly endangered species. Many turtles die from swallowing plastic bags because they mistake them for jellyfish.

PLAY AND LEARN!

The **LEATHERBACK SEA TURTLE** lays its eggs...

- on beaches

- in woods

- in burrows

It lives in...

- rivers

- sea

- lakes

It loves...

- shellfish

- jellyfish

- fish

© STEVE BYLAND - FOTOLIA

© JIMMY - FOTOLIA

© MARLENE GREENE - FOTOLIA

© PHILIP PULEO - ISTOCKPHOTO

© DDECHAMPS - FOTOLIA

© ADDYTSL - SHUTTERSTOCK

© CHRIS HILL - FOTOLIA

© ANDREAS GRADIN - FOTOLIA

© TASHA LAVIGNE - FOTOLIA

FOREST ANIMALS

THE STRIPED SKUNK

Identity Card

Up to 2 ft. 11 in. (65 cm) in length

Up to 14 lbs. (6.3 kg)

● Wind Cave National Park, South Dakota
■ Zone range

WHAT IS IT?

The STRIPED SKUNK is black with two long white stripes on its back and a very bushy, white tail. It is a pretty mammal, closely related to the weasel family.

WHERE DOES IT LIVE AND WHAT DOES IT EAT?

The STRIPED SKUNK retreats into its den in the day and comes out at night. Its habitat can be forests, farmland, or city outskirts. It feeds on little animals, eggs, and fruit.

HOW DOES IT DEFEND ITSELF?

The STRIPED SKUNK's reputation as a foul-smelling animal is because it sprays any potential enemy with a strong, unpleasant liquid secreted by its anal scent glands. The smell is not only awful... it also lasts for quite some time!

USEFUL TO KNOW...

The STRIPED SKUNK is very common and can be seen in suburban and urban areas.

PLAY AND LEARN!

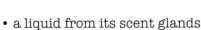

The **STRIPED SKUNK** defends itself with...

- a liquid from its scent glands

- whip-like movements with its tail

- its claws

It is especially active...

- in the sun

- when it rains

- at night

It is...

- striped

- spotted

- black with two white stripes

Identity Card

Up to 2 ft. 11 in. (65 cm) in length

Up to 30.86 lbs. (14 kg)

● Yellowstone National Park, Wyoming, Montana and Idaho
■ Zone range

WHAT IS IT?

The PORCUPINE is a rodent. Its coat is a mixture of hair, bristles, fur, and 30,000 very sharp, brown quills! It has a big body and strong claws.

WHERE AND HOW DOES IT LIVE?

The PORCUPINE lives mostly in forests and bushes. Although it is slow, it is agile and spends a lot of time in treetops. Its main diet is the bark and leaves of trees.

IS IT DANGEROUS?

This solitary rodent, protected by its sharp quills, is a peaceful animal. However, if it is attacked, the PORCUPINE will stick its quills into its aggressor, causing serious injury.

USEFUL TO KNOW...

The PORCUPINE has natural antibiotics, which prevent it from seriously harming itself with its own quills. This species is common.

PLAY AND LEARN!

The PORCUPINE is carnivorous.

- True
- False

It lives in treetops.

- True
- False

It defends itself with its teeth.

- True
- False

It has strong claws.

- True

- False

THE WOOD FROG

Identity Card

Up to 2.75 in. (70 mm) in length.

Up to 0.71 oz. (20 grams)

● Gates of the Arctic National Park, Alaska
■ Zone range

WHAT IS IT?

The WOOD FROG is brown or gray but never green and its smooth skin must always remain moist. It can make impressive leaps thanks to its powerful hind legs.

WHAT DOES IT EAT?

Like all frogs, the WOOD FROG is extremely voracious. It feeds on insects, worms, and spiders.

WHERE DOES IT LIVE?

The WOOD FROG lives in cool and damp forests. It hibernates for a long time in winter. In the spring, the female lays more than 1,000 eggs in woodland ponds.

USEFUL TO KNOW...

The WOOD FROG lives in very cold places in winter. To withstand the cold, some parts of its body actually freeze during the hibernation period. When spring arrives, its body thaws and it returns to normal life!

PLAY AND LEARN!

The WOOD FROG lives in...

• damp forests

• grassland

• prairies

Its skin is...

• covered with scales

• smooth

• full of pustules

It can lay up to...

• 10 eggs

• 1,000 eggs

• 10,000 eggs

Identity Card

13.8 in.
(35 cm)

Up to 8.8 oz.
(250 grams)

● Wind Cave National Park, South Dakota
■ Zone range

WHAT IS IT?

The AMERICAN RED SQUIRREL is an agile creature with a slender body and a long, bushy tail. This rodent has very sharp teeth, which are very useful for cracking open nuts and hard fruit.

WHERE DOES IT LIVE?

The AMERICAN RED SQUIRREL lives in forests. It makes its drey (nest) in the hole of a tree or under a stack of leaves. In winter, it rarely ventures out of its drey.

WHAT DOES IT EAT?

The AMERICAN RED SQUIRREL spends a lot of time on the ground, foraging for seeds or mushrooms.

USEFUL TO KNOW...

In the fall, the AMERICAN RED SQUIRREL's coat changes color so it can blend into its surroundings. Its back turns gray and its underside is white.

PLAY AND LEARN!

The RED SQUIRREL hibernates.

- True
- False

It uses its tail to swim.

- True
- False

It lives in trees.

- True
- False

It lives in the North Pole.

- True
- False

THE GRAY WOLF

© KAREL BROZ – ISTOCKPHOTO

Identity Card

 36 – 63 in. (90 – 160 cm)

 40 – 175 lbs. (18 – 80 kg)

● Wood Buffalo National Park, Alberta (Canada)
■ Zone range

WHAT IS IT?

The GRAY WOLF is an ancestor of the dog, but its head is bigger and its teeth are stronger and sharper. It is a carnivorous mammal. The color of its coat varies from gray to brown.

HOW DOES IT TRAVEL?

When GRAY WOLVES go hunting, they always travel in single file and can cover vast distances of about 400 square miles (1,000 km²).

HOW DOES IT LIVE AND WHAT DOES IT EAT?

GRAY WOLVES live in packs. Together, they help each other hunt, face danger, and protect the cubs from any predators. The GRAY WOLF eats deer, small mammals, and berries.

WHAT ARE BABY WOLVES LIKE?

The GRAY WOLF's cubs are blind at birth and do not stand up until they are at least ten days old.

PLAY AND LEARN!

The GRAY WOLF eats...

• vegetables

• meat

• everything

Its cubs are...

• blind at birth

• white at birth

• hairless

It has...

• sharp teeth

• fins

• quills

Identity Card

7 – 9 in.
(18 – 23 cm)

1.4 – 2 oz.
(39 – 56 grams)

- Great Smoky Mountains National Park, Tennessee and North Carolina
- Zone range

WHAT IS IT?

The RED-COCKADED WOODPECKER is a medium-sized bird. On its back are black and white horizontal stripes. Its most distinguishing feature is a black cap and nape that encircle large white cheek patches.

WHERE DOES IT LIVE?

The RED-COCKADED WOODPECKER makes its home in mature pine forests. However, the destruction of that habitat has resulted in the woodpecker becoming an endangered species.

WHERE DOES ITS NAME COME FROM?

Males are the only one to have a small red streak on each side of its black cap called a cockade, hence its name. In the 18th century, "cockade" was regularly used to refer to a ribbon or other ornament worn on a hat.

WHAT IS ITS DIET?

It feeds primarily on ants, beetles, caterpillars, insects, and spiders, and occasionally fruit and berries.

PLAY AND LEARN!

Its height is at least 20 inches.

- True
- False

Only females have a black "cockade."

- True
- False

They mostly live in pine trees.

- True
- False

They eat fish like all birds.

- True

- False

THE ELK

Identity Card

(Height at the shoulder)
4 to 5 ft.
(1.20 m – 1.50 m)

325 to 1,100 lbs.
(150 – 500 kg)

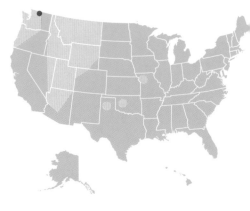

● North Cascades National Park, Washington
■ Zone range

WHAT IS IT?

The ELK is one of the largest species of deer in the world. This animal should not be confused with the larger moose.

WHY DO ELK MIGRATE?

In early summer, ELK migrate to high mountain grazing grounds where the cows (females) will give birth. The herds return to lower valley pastures where they eat shrubs or paw through snow to graze on grass.

DO THEY HAVE ANOTHER NAME?

ELK are also called wapiti, a Native American word that means "light-colored deer."

USEFUL TO KNOW...

The ELK have four stomachs because of the complicated process they use to digest food. Their diets vary somewhat depending on the season, and include: native grasses, tree bark (in winter), and tree sprouts (during the summer).

PLAY AND LEARN!

ELK feed on...

• small mammals like mice

• grass

• rabbits

They migrate to high mountains to...

• find more food

• give birth

• hibernate

What other name are they called?

• A mooth

• A deer

• A wapiti

THE CHIPMUNK

Identity Card

 4 to 7 in.
(10 – 17 cm)

1 – 5 oz.
(28 – 140 grams)

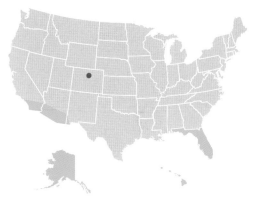

● Rocky Mountain National Park, Colorado
■ Zone range

WHAT IS IT?

CHIPMUNKS are small, striped squirrels. They have pudgy cheeks, large, glossy eyes, and bushy tails. They have contrasting dark and light stripes on the sides of their faces and across their backs and tails.

HOW DO THEY HUNT FOR FOOD?

CHIPMUNKS generally gather food on the ground in areas with underbrush, rocks, and logs. They feed on insects, nuts, berries, seeds, fruit, and grains, which they stuff into their generous cheek pouches and carry to their burrow or nest to store.

DO THEY HIBERNATE?

CHIPMUNKS hibernate during winter. Usually hibernating animals store fat; chipmunks periodically dip into their cache of nuts and seeds throughout the winter.

DO THEY LIVE IN LARGE GROUPS?

CHIPMUNKS are solitary creatures and normally ignore one another except during the spring, when mating takes place.

PLAY AND LEARN!

CHIPMUNKS feed on...

- mice
- insects
- grass

Why do they hibernate?

- To stock fat
- To rest
- To dip into their nuts

They gather food... and carry it.

- on their paws
- on their back
- in their mouth

THE CANADA LYNX

Identity Card

35.4 – 43.3 in.
(90 – 110 cm)

Up to 37.4 lbs.
(17 kg)

● Yoho National Park, British Columbia (Canada
■ Zone range

■ WHAT IS IT?

The CANADA LYNX is a feline, and is well adapted to extremely cold conditions. It has a dense coat and big tufts of fur on its feet, which prevent it from sinking into the snow. Its tail is short and it has curious furry tufts on its ears.

■ HOW DOES IT LIVE?

The CANADA LYNX is a solitary animal that travels through northern forests in search of food. In the winter, it has to travel great distances to satisfy its hunger.

■ HOW DOES IT ATTRACT A FEMALE?

The males make very high-pitched calls, which sound like wails. The female replies to these calls with little howls.

■ HOW DOES IT HUNT?

The CANADA LYNX is silent and moves with great agility. It is also endowed with excellent vision. When hunting, it stalks its prey, crawls towards it, then leaps upon it in one bound.

PLAY AND LEARN!

The **CANADA LYNX** has...

• a short tail

• a long tail

• no tail

It has small tufts of fur on...

• its ears

• its paws

• its nose

What kind of sounds does it make?

• It makes no sound

• It roars

• It makes high-pitched calls

THE MOOSE

Identity Card

Up to 7 ft. 6 in. to its withers (2.30 m)

Up to 1,800 lbs. (815 kg)

- Yoho National Park, British Columbia (Canada)
- Zone range

■ WHAT IS IT?

The MOOSE belongs to the deer family and is recognizable by its long legs and big, flat antlers. It has a dark brown or gray coat and palmed hooves, enabling it to swim very well and to travel over swampy land.

■ WHERE DOES IT LIVE AND WHAT DOES IT EAT?

The MOOSE lives in large, northern forests and marshes. It can live on its own or as a pair. This animal loves swimming. It feeds on grass, leaves, and aquatic plants.

■ IS IT DOMESTICATED?

In Asia, MOOSE have been domesticated for many centuries. However, given that it is a wild and solitary animal, it is not easy to tame, unlike the caribou.

■ USEFUL TO KNOW...

During breeding season, the MOOSE is very hostile and can be bad-tempered and dangerous.

PLAY AND LEARN!

The MOOSE belongs to the bear family.

- True

- False

It lives in forests and swamps.

- True

- False

It is easy to identify by its big, flat antlers.

- True

- False

It gathers together in huge herds.

- True

- False

THE RACCOON

Identity Card

15.5 – 25 in.
(40 – 60 cm)

9 – 20 lbs.
(4 – 9 kg)

- Cuyahoga Valley National Park, Ohio
- Zone range

WHAT IS IT?

The RACCOON is a mammal with a grayish coat and a distinctive black "mask" on its face. It has a black and yellow gray striped tail, which measures 29.8 inches (75 cm).

DOES IT ADAPT EASILY?

Due to its capacity to adapt, the RACCOON can live in many different places, including suburban gardens.

WHERE DOES ITS NAME COME FROM AND WHAT DOES IT EAT?

Its name comes from a Native American word meaning "the one who scratches with its hands" because the RACCOON carefully washes its food before eating it. This animal feeds on fish, clams, crayfish, fruit, and nuts.

WHAT DOES IT DO IN WINTER?

The RACCOON's body stores fat reserves on which it survives during hibernation. However, this animal does not really hibernate; it has more of a long, winter rest.

PLAY AND LEARN!

The RACCOON has a dark mask on its face.

- True
- False

It cleans its food carefully.

- True
- False

It has a striped tail.

- True
- False

It can be found in gardens.

- True

- False

© JUSTIMAGINE (RAMBLEON) - FOTOLIA

© RBBRDCKYBK (BILL KENNEDY) - FOTOLIA

© JAMES PIERCE - SHUTTERSTOCK

© HILDEBRAND PHOTOGRAPHY - ISTOCKPHOTO

© TOM HIRTREITER - FOTOLIA

© RONNIE HOWARD - FOTOLIA

© BRUCE MACQUEEN - FOTOLIA

© SYDNEY ALVARES - FOTOLIA

© CHRISTIAN MUSAT - FOTOLIA

BIRDS

THE RUBY-THROATED HUMMINGBIRD

Identity Card

Up to 3.5 in. (9 cm) in length, including the beak

Less than 0.14 oz. (4 grams)

- Shenandoah National Park, Virginia
- Zone range

WHAT IS IT?

The RUBY-THROATED HUMMINGBIRD has been given this name because the male's throat is deep red in color. Its beak is very long and slender.

WHERE DOES IT LIVE?

The RUBY-THROATED HUMMINGBIRD lives in forests, parks, and gardens. In winter, it migrates to Mexico or Central America and returns to North America in the spring. It builds its little nest in treetops.

WHAT DOES IT EAT?

Like all hummingbirds, it uses its long beak to collect the nectar from flowers. It also eats many insects.

USEFUL TO KNOW...

Hummingbirds are small birds that can flap their wings very fast, up to 75 times per second when hovering!

PLAY AND LEARN!

This HUMMINGBIRD always has a red...

- beak
- throat
- eye

It feeds on...

- nectar
- seeds
- fish

Where does it migrate in winter?

- East
- North
- South

Identity Card

2 ft. 1 in. (65 cm) in length

Up to 2.13 lbs. (1.kg)

● Acadia National Park, Maine
■ Zone range

WHAT IS IT?
The HERRING GULL is a large, white and gray bird with an orange beak. It can be seen gliding above the shores or resting on rocks.

IS IT NOISY?
The HERRING GULL is very noisy. Its distinct call is one of the sounds that can be heard most at the seashore. It squawks loudly to indicate its presence and defend its territory.

WHAT DOES IT EAT?
The HERRING GULL is a very greedy bird! It feeds mostly on fish, but at low tide, it can be seen searching for shellfish among the rocks.

USEFUL TO KNOW...
The HERRING GULL is a social bird that lives in colonies. It is a very common bird and is often spotted in coastal towns.

PLAY AND LEARN!

The HERRING GULL is a very noisy bird.

• True

• False

It is all white.

• True

• False

It also lives in cities.

• True

• False

It is a solitary bird.

• True

• False

THE NORTHERN CARDINAL

Identity Card

Up to 9 in. in length
(23 cm)

Up to 1.7 oz.
(48 grams)

- Saguaro National Park, Arizona
- Zone range

WHAT IS IT?

The male NORTHERN CARDINAL has a bright, crimson plumage so that despite being a little bird, it is very eye-catching! The name "cardinal" is a reference to cardinals of the Catholic Church who wear red robes.

WHERE DOES IT LIVE AND WHAT DOES IT EAT?

This bird, which belongs to the passerine family, lives in pairs. It can be found in woodland trees and shrubs and in swamps. Its main diet is seeds, fruit, and insects.

IS IT A GOOD SINGER?

The NORTHERN CARDINAL sings beautifully. Its tuneful song varies from region to region. The male sings to mark its territory and to attract females.

USEFUL TO KNOW...

These birds usually breed twice a year and the female lays three or four eggs per clutch (a group of eggs). While she sits on the eggs, the male feeds her beak-to-beak.

PLAY AND LEARN!

The male CARDINAL is bright red.

- True
- False

It feeds on small animals.

- True
- False

It is an ocean bird.

- True
- False

It lives in pairs.

- True
- False

THE SNOWY OWL

Identity Card

Up to 2 ft. 3 in. (70 cm)

From 3 to 3.5 lbs. (1.5 – 1.6 kg)

• Wapusk National Park, Manitoba (Canada)
■ Zone range

WHAT IS IT?
The SNOWY OWL is a diurnal (daytime) bird. Its wingspan can measure up to 5 ft. 8 in. (1.75 m) and its feathered feet protect it from the cold.

WHERE DOES IT BUILD ITS NEST?
The SNOWY OWL lives in the Arctic regions. It builds its nest on bare ground between moss-covered mounds.

WHAT IS ITS PLUMAGE LIKE?
The SNOWY OWL has speckled, white and black feathers. In winter, it turns all white to blend with the snow and become less visible to predators.

HOW DOES IT HUNT?
Unlike other owls, the SNOWY OWL hunts mostly during the day, using its sharp talons to capture its prey.

PLAY AND LEARN!

The SNOWY OWL builds its nest between mounds.

• True

• False

It has thick feathers on its feet.

• True

• False

Its plumage is black.

• True

• False

It hunts only at night.

• True

• False

THE AMERICAN ROBIN

Identity Card

Up to 11 in.
(28 cm) in length

Up to 1.05 oz.
(30 grams)

● Grand Teton National Park, Wyoming
■ Zone range

PLAY AND LEARN!

■ WHAT IS IT?
The AMERICAN ROBIN has a pretty coloring, including a reddish-orange breast and belly, a black head, and gray feathers. This bird belongs to the passerine family.

■ WHERE DOES IT LIVE AND WHAT DOES IT EAT?
In winter, the AMERICAN ROBIN lives in flocks of up to 250,000 birds! Its habitat is forests, farmland, and towns. It feeds on insects, fruit, and, especially, earthworms.

■ HOW DOES IT BREED?
In the spring, this migratory bird travels to cooler regions to breed. It builds a solid nest, made of twigs smeared with mud, in a tree.

■ USEFUL TO KNOW...
The AMERICAN ROBIN is also known as a Robin or a Robin Redbreast.

The AMERICAN ROBIN's tail is red.

- True
- False

It lives with one mate.

- True
- False

It only eats seeds.

- True
- False

It stays in the same place.

- True
- False

Identity Card

3.2 – 4.5 ft.
(1 – 1.4 m)

4.6 – 7.3 lbs.
(2 – 3.5 kg)

● Cuyahoga Valley National Park, Ohio
■ Zone range

■ WHAT IS IT?

The GREAT BLUE HERON is a wading bird that walks slowly through shallow waters on its long, spindly legs. The two long feathers on its head are known as the crest.

■ HOW DOES IT LIVE?

This aquatic bird uses its long bill to dig up fish and other aquatic animals in the silt of lakes or river banks. It is an excellent flyer, and in winter, it migrates much further south.

■ HOW DOES IT BREED?

The GREAT BLUE HERON often lives in colonies. The female lays her eggs in a nest built among aquatic plants.

■ USEFUL TO KNOW...

The GREAT BLUE HERON is the largest North American aquatic bird. It is often seen in the many lakes of Quebec, Canada.

PLAY AND LEARN!

It lives in wetlands.

- True
- False

It has two horns on its head.

- True
- False

It is a solitary bird.

- True
- False

It can only be seen swimming in the ocean.

- True
- False

THE BLUE JAY

Identity Card

Up to 11.8 in. (30 cm) in length

Up to 4.2 oz. (120 grams)

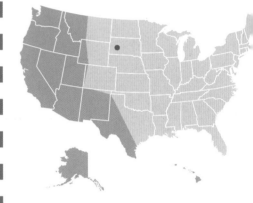

● Badlands National Park, South Dakota
■ Zone range

WHAT IS IT?

The plumage of the BLUE JAY is blue or lavender-blue. The black band around its throat looks like a necklace. Its straight and slender bill is very useful for searching for food.

WHERE DOES IT LIVE?

The natural habitat of the BLUE JAY is normally forests, but it is now also found in city parks and gardens. It either lives alone or forms a pair.

WHAT DOES IT EAT?

The BLUE JAY is mostly a grain-eating bird; it likes seeds and acorns but is also fond of insects. It is known to attack small animals, including other birds, rodents, and bats!

USEFUL TO KNOW...

The BLUE JAY has a very high-pitched call, which it repeats two or three times. It can also mimic the calls of other birds.

PLAY AND LEARN!

The BLUE JAY lives in a group.

- True
- False

It eats seeds and fruits.

- True
- False

The sound it makes is soft.

- True
- False

It repeats its call.

- True
- False

 Up to 3 ft. 3 in. (1 m);
wingspan: 7 ft. 2 in. (2.2 m)

 6.5 lbs. (3 kg) – 14.5 lbs. (6.5 kg)

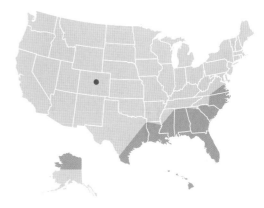

● Rocky Mountain National Park, Colorado
■ Zone range

WHAT IS IT?

The GOLDEN EAGLE is a superb, majestic bird of prey. It has a hooked beak, very sharp talons, and broad wings with tapering feathers. The color of its plumage depends on its age.

WHERE DOES IT LIVE?

This bird of prey lives mostly in the mountains. Its excellent eyesight is useful for spotting prey, which it hunts in the day. The GOLDEN EAGLE lives in pairs and often builds its aerie (nest) on an inaccessible rock face.

WHAT DOES IT EAT?

The GOLDEN EAGLE is a formidable predator that feeds on mammals and other birds. It is capable of capturing a sheep.

USEFUL TO KNOW...

The GOLDEN EAGLE is the king of all birds and symbolizes power and courage ever since antiquity. This bird of prey does not attack man.

PLAY AND LEARN!

The GOLDEN EAGLE is a night bird.

- True
- False

Its main diet consists of mammals.

- True
- False

It lives on the coast.

- True
- False

It is the symbol of power and courage.

- True
- False

THE GREATER FLAMINGO

Identity Card

4 ft. 6 in. – 5 ft.
(1.4 – 1.5 m)

4.5 – 8.5 lbs
(2 – 4 kg)

● Everglades National Park, Florida
■ Zone range

■ WHAT IS IT?
The GREATER FLAMINGO is a tall bird measuring at least 4 ft. 11 inches (1.5 m) with long legs and a long neck. It has a curved bill, a small head, and pink and white feathers.

■ HOW DOES IT FEED ITS CHICKS?
Female FLAMINGOS feed their chicks by regurgitating a sort of "milk" or "soup" that they have previously swallowed.

■ HOW DOES IT LIVE?
The GREATER FLAMINGO lives in big colonies or flocks. During the mating season and migrating period, the flocks greatly increase in size.

■ WHY IS IT PINK?
The GREATER FLAMINGO has pink feathers because of a pigment present in the freshwater shrimp on which it feeds.

PLAY AND LEARN!

The **GREATER FLAMINGO** eats shrimps.

- True
- False

It is red.

- True
- False

Its legs are chubby.

- True
- False

It lives in flocks.

- True
- False

GAMES

HAVE FUN...

DESERT ANIMALS

1. I live a solitary life. I can leap three meters (9 ft. 10 in.) high and I am all white in winter. Who am I?
2. What is the meaning of "COYOTE"?

MOUNTAIN ANIMALS

3. What does the GROUNDHOG do when it runs out of food?
4. I am a solitary animal. I like salmon and I sleep a lot in winter. Who am I?
5. Which animal can fly 3.7 miles (6,000 meters) high?

RIVER AND LAKE ANIMALS

6. What does the WOOD TURTLE eat?
7. Why is the STURGEON an endangered species?
8. I live near the lakeside. I have big claws but I am an aquatic herbivore. Who am I?
9. Which animal is becoming extinct?
10. Why does the BULLFROG have this name?

SEA ANIMALS

11. What is the biggest animal on Earth?
12. Which sea mammal is very playful but also aggressive?
13. I am a crustacean with a black and orange shell and I swim backwards. Who am I?
14. What is the particularity of the SWORDFISH?
15. Which animal was named after a famous naturalist?

PRAIRIE ANIMALS

16. My stripes are black and white and my skin is soft. Who am I?
17. Which animal is a cousin of the cow?
18. Which snake is totally harmless?
19. Which mammal is a cousin of the lynx?

FOREST ANIMALS

20. What does the PORCUPINE use to defend itself?
21. How many eggs does the female WOOD FROG lay in the spring?
22. What is the distinctive feature of the CANADA LYNX?
23. Which animal can change color to blend in with the forest?

BIRDS

24. Why does the RUBY-THROATED HUMMINGBIRD have this name?
25. Why is the CARDINAL so easy to see?
26. What is the other name given to the SNOWY OWL?
27. I am blue and I search for food with my straight and slender beak.
    I am also very chatty. Who am I?
28. Which animal is the symbol of power and courage?

THERE ARE 7 DIFFERENCES IN THE DRAWING...

MAPS OF THE NATIONAL PARKS

Olympic

North Cascades

Glacier

Theodore Roosevelt

Bighorn Canyon National Recreation Area

Voyageurs

Mount Rainier

Cuyahoga Valley

Acadia

Wind Cave

Yellowstone

Pt Reyes National Seashore

Yosemite

Grand Teton

Badlands

Great Basin

Bryce Canyon

Rocky Mountain

Shenandoah

Channel Islands

Canyonlands

Great Sand Dunes

Mammoth Cave

Grand Canyon

Great Smoky Mountains

Death Valley

Joshua Tree

Congaree

Saguaro

Canaveral National Seashore

Big Bend

Hot Springs

Biscayne

Padre Island Seashore

Denali

Gates of the Arctic

Everglades

Kenai Fjords

Glacier Bay

Hawaii Volcanoes

Virgin Islands

MAPS OF THE NATIONAL PARKS

Quttinirpaaq

Vuntut

Kluane

Auyuittuq

Wood Buffalo

Torngat Mountains

Ukkusiksalik

Terra Nova

Wapusk

Yoho

Cape Breton
Highlands

Prince Albert

Riding Mountain

La Mauricie

Kejimkujik

Point Pelee

ANSWERS

DESERT ANIMALS

Page 8 – The Coyote: true – false – true – false
Page 9 – The Desert Tortoise: 1 (in the form of a dome) – 2 (grass and herbs) – 2 (brown)
Page 10 – The Kangaroo Rat: true – true – true – false
Page 11 – The Jackrabbit: false – false – false – true
Page 12 – The Raven: 3 (black feathers) – 2 (everything they can find) – 2 (three eggs)
Page 13 – The Roadrunner: false – true – true – true
Page 14 – The Sidewinder: 2 (its fangs) – 3 (sandy and rocky deserts) – 3 (sideways)
Page 15 – The Scorpion: 1 (under a rock) – 3 (on its tail) – 1 (spiders)
Page 16 – The Gila Monster: true – true – true – false
Page 17 – The Canyon Bat: 1 (in small group) – 1 (tiny) – 1 (flying insects)
Page 18 – The Pronghorn: false – true – false – true

RIVER AND LAKE ANIMALS

Page 20 – The American Beaver: 2 (like a rudder) – 2 (trees) – 2 (near water)
Page 21 – The Wood Turtle: 2 (in rivers and ponds) – 2 (in humid undergrowth) – 1 (sculpted and brown)
Page 22 – The Bullfrog: 2 (the roar of the bull) – 1 (in rivers and lakes) – 3 (by its big eardrums)
Page 23 – The American Alligator: true – false – true – false
Page 24 – The Crocodile: true – false – true – false
Page 25 – The Salmon: false – true – false – true
Page 26 – The River Otter: 3 (mammal) – 1 (the water) – 2 (smooth)
Page 27 – The Sturgeon: false – false – false – true
Page 28 – The Florida Manatee: 3 (mammal) – 2 (warm coastal waters) – 2 (seaweed and sea grass)

MOUNTAIN ANIMALS

Page 30 – The Bighorn Sheep: false – true – true – true
Page 31 – The Grizzly Bear: 1 (in its hind paws) – 2 (water) – 2 (his claws)
Page 32 – The Yellow-Bellied Marmot: 3 (into hibernation) – 3 (grass) – 1 (deep)
Page 33 – The Cougar: true – true – true – true
Page 34 – The Black Bear: true – false – false – false
Page 35 – The Mountain Kingsnake: false – true –false –true
Page 36 – The California Condor: true – true – false – true
Page 37 – The Wild Turkey: false – false – false – false
Page 38 – The Red Fox: 1 (in the forest) – 1 (hens) – 1 (red)
Page 39 – The Great Horned Owl: 3 (short and stocky body) – 2 (mammals) – 2 (two tufts of feathers)
Page 40 – The Peregrine Falcon: 1 (an excellent vision) – 2 (North America) – 1 (a white down)

PRAIRIE ANIMALS

Page 42 – The Bobcat: 1 (good hunters) – 2 (pointy ears) – 3 (lynx)
Page 43 – The Common Garter Snake: false – true – false – false
Page 44 – The Smooth Green Snake: true – false – false – true
Page 45 – The Spotted Salamander: 2 (shiny skin) – 2 (water) – 1 (whole body)
Page 46 – The Prairie Dog: false – true – true – true
Page 47 – The American Bison: 2 (cow) – 3 (prairies) – 3 (lives in herd)
Page 48 – The Black-Footed Ferret: true – true – true – true
Page 49 – The Badger: 3 (birds) – 3 (only one) – 1 (white)
Page 50 – The Least Weasel: 3 (everywhere in the world) – 1 (small rodents) – 2 (prairies)

ANSWERS

SEA ANIMALS

Page 52 – The Blue Whale: 1 (mammal) – 2 (cold waters) – 2 (songs)
Page 53 – The Humpback Whale: false – true – false – false
Page 54 – The Harbor Seal: false – true – false – true
Page 55 – The Atlantic Lobster: 2 (crustacean) – 2 (in the ocean among the rocks) – 3 (its black and orange carapace)
Page 56 – The Great White Shark: 1 (a fish) – 3 (seals) – 3 (coastal waters)
Page 57 – The Elephant Seal: 1 (328 feet) – 2 (short) – 2 (its back)
Page 58 – The Steller Sea Lion: true – false – true – true
Page 59 – The Swordfish: 2 (warm waters) – 2 (to hunt fish) – 3 (up to 9 years)
Page 60 – The Gray Whale: false – false – true – true
Page 61 – The Manta Ray: 2 (thick cartilage) – 3 (in warm waters) – 2 (at the surface of the ocean)
Page 62 – The Leatherback Sea Turtle: 1 (on beaches) – 2 (sea) – 2 (jellyfish)

FOREST ANIMALS

Page 64 – The Striped Skunk: 1 (a liquid from its glands) – 3 (at night) – 3 (black with two white stripes)
Page 65 – The Porcupine: false – true – false – true
Page 66 – The Wood Frog: 1(damp forests) – 2 (smooth) – 2 (1,000 eggs)
Page 67 – The American Red Squirrel: true – false – true – false
Page 68 – The Gray Wolf: 2 (meats) – 1 (blind at birth) – 1 (sharp teeth)
Page 69 – The Red-Cockaded Woodpecker: false – false – true – false
Page 70 – The Elk: 2 (grass) – 2 (to give birth) – 3 (a wapiti)
Page 71 – The Chipmunk: 2 (insects) – 3 (to dip into their nuts) – 3 (in their mouth)
Page 72 – The Canada Lynx: 1 (a short tail) – 1 (its ears) – 3 (it makes high-pitched calls)
Page 73 – The Moose: false – true – true – false
Page 74 – The Raccoon: true – true – true – true

BIRDS

Page 76 – The Ruby-Throated Hummingbird: 2 (throat) – 1 (nectar) – 3 (south)
Page 77 – The Herring Gull: true – false – true – false
Page 78 – The Northern Cardinal: true – false – false – true
Page 79 – The Snowy Owl: true – true – false – false
Page 80 – The American Robin: false – false – false – false
Page 81 – The Great Blue Heron: true – false – false – true
Page 82 – The Blue Jay: false – true – false – true
Page 83 – The Golden Eagle: false – true – false – true
Page 84 – The Greater Flamingo: true – true – false – true

HAVE FUN WHILE TESTING YOUR KNOWLEDGE

1. The jackrabbit - 2. It means the "one that howls" - 3. Its heartbeat slows down
4. The grizzly bear - 5. The California condor - 6. The wood turtle feeds on plants and food
7. The sturgeon is endangered because they produce caviar - 8. I am the Florida manatee
9. The wood turtle is becoming extinct - 10. Because its sound is the same as the bull's roar
11. The blue whale - 12. The harbor seal - 13. The Atlantic lobster
14. Its long and flat bill - 15. The steller sea lion - 16. The striped skunk
17. The American bison - 18. The smooth green snake
19. The bobcat - 20. Its sharp quills - 21. 1,000 eggs - 22. The Canada lynx has excellent vision
23. The red squirrel - 24. Because of the color of its throat - 25. Because its coat is bright red
26. snow goose - 27. The blue jay - 28. The golden eagle